To

FERNANDO PE

The Surprise of being

James Greene has translated selections of the Russian poets Mandelstam (with forewords by Nadezhda Mandelstam and Donald Davie, Elek, 1977; revised and expanded edition Granada, 1980) and, with Cynthia Westwood, A. Fet (*I have come to you to greet you*, Angel, 1982); and, with Robin Fulton and Siv Hennum, of the Norwegian poet Olav Hauge (*Don't give me the whole truth*, Anvil, 1985). His versions of Mandelstam have been read at the National Theatre, the Mermaid Theatre, Riverside Studios, the Oxford and Cambridge Poetry Festivals, and on Radio 3; three of them are included in *The Oxford Book of Verse in English Translation*, edited by Charles Tomlinson (1980). He is the author of *Dead-man's-fall* (poems; the Bodley Head, 1980).

Clara de Azevedo Mafra was born in Lisbon and emigrated to London in 1964. She is a painter.

Jaime H. da Silva is Assistant Professor of Portuguese at the University of Puerto Rico.

FERNANDO PESSOA

The Surprise of Being

Twenty-five poems translated by
James Greene and Clara de Azevedo Mafra

Dual text

ANGEL BOOKS
LONDON

First published by Angel Books, 3 Kelross Road,
London N5 2QS

Translations copyright © James Greene
and Clara de Azevedo Mafra 1986
Introduction copyright © Angel Books 1986

3 5 7 9 10 8 6 4

British Library Cataloguing in Publication Data

Pessoa, Fernando
    The surprise of being: twenty-five poems.
    I. Title II. Greene, James, 1938 –
    III. Azevedo Mafra, Clara de
    869. 1'4 PQ9261.P417

    ISBN 0-946162-23-9
    ISBN 0-946162-24-7 Pbk

ACKNOWLEDGEMENTS

Portuguese texts are those of *Obras completas
de Fernando Pessoa*, edited by João Caspar
Simões and Luís de Montalvor, Atica, Lisbon
1980.

We should like to thank David Black, Robert
Chandler, Jaime H. da Silva, and Antony
Wood for their critical comments.

Typeset in Great Britain by Trintype,
printed and bound by Woolnough Bookbinding,
both of Irthlingborough, Northants

I am like a room with innumerable
fantastic mirrors that distort into false
reflections a unique previous reality;
which isn't in any and is in all of them.

My heart is a broken portico,
Too much overlooking the sea.
I see in my soul the vain sails go by
And each sail goes in its own direction . . .

FERNANDO PESSOA

*translated by James Greene
and Clara de Azevedo Mafra*

Contents

Contents

Introduction

Few poets have had the fortuitous burden of bearing a surname that so encapsulates the essence of their poetic unfolding as has Fernando Pessoa. Derived from the Latin *persona*, denoting the mask used in the Roman theatre, and originally from the verb *personare*, 'to sound through', the Portuguese word *pessoa* connotes a multiplicity of meanings which place Fernando Antonio Pessoa at the centre of European Modernism's reworking of a perceived disintegration of Western culture and of the post-Romantic 'I'.

Through a fragmentation of his Self into well delineated other selves – 'heteronyms' as Pessoa labels them, a neologism based on the Greek for 'other name' – the poet elevates himself to a Godhead whose literary, non-biblical 'genesis', as he describes it in a manifesto-letter to a coeval critic and admirer, is a counter-Creation. Yet this expansion of the poetic universe leaves a void – 'God has no unity/How am I to be one?' – which is the 'orthonym', Pessoa, when he writes in his own name. Hence, it is behind and through *that* mask that the artificer-poet practises his aesthetic of *depersonalisation*. Upon each heteronym, the creator places a *persona* with attendant biography, world-view, civil status, and even physical details; into Caeiro, Campos and Reis – the principal figures in this 'drama in persons, not in acts' – the poetic life-force is inspired and as the masks in Roman theatre also served to augment the volume of the actors' speech, each distinct style adds a scriptural voice to the now sacralised compilation that is Pessoa's opus.

However, the one *persona* which is never fixed is that of Pessoa, the orthonym. Born in Lisbon in 1888, orphaned at an early age and educated in South Africa at an English high school thanks to his stepfather's position (his father died when he was five) as Portuguese consul, Pessoa repatriated himself in 1905 and lived in Lisbon for the rest of his life. Though he took an active part in the renaissance in Portuguese poetry that began around 1910, publishing critical essays and verse in flamboyant style that suited the new movements such as Futurism, little of his poetry was published in his lifetime and it was only after his death that his true stature was recognised. He earned his living as a commercial translator of correspondence in English and French. Despite, or perhaps because of, his biographical and social identity, the orthonym is the most stylistically varied and least stable of Pessoa's poetic non-persons. His poetry is always a flight from personality, from philosophical and intellectual certitude, from the norms of speech and syntax, and from any feeling or passion not imagined.

In this perpetual flux, Pessoa stands in opposition to each of the heteronyms. Alberto Caeiro is the 'naive poet that every poet wishes he could be', as Octavio Paz has characterised him: a poet with no literary background; a believer in natural religion, in the objectivity of his senses; and a practitioner of free verse unembellished by metaphors or similes which are 'lies'. He is the primal poet because he is a natural bard; or, in a post-Romantic era, an anti-poet. Ricardo Reis affirms the priority of the Graeco-Roman deities over their latter-day Christian parodies; he finds himself misplaced in the twentieth century and is estranged even from his own language which he endeavours to re-latinise.

He has been in self-imposed exile in Brazil, intellectually and linguistically, as well as politically, since 1919 after the failure of the last monarchist uprising in Republican Portugal. And Álvaro de Campos, the cosmopolitan, multi-lingual naval engineer educated in Glasgow, reader of *The Times*, after reading Walt Whitman abandons his fin-de-siècle decadence to embark upon a phase of Futurist exuberance, only to lapse exhausted into a final period of existentialist angst.

Although fictive creations of someone known to us as Fernando Pessoa, the individual voices of these *personae* are always clearer and more identifiable than that of the orthonym. All four are in a constant dynamic complement to each other, often alluding to and contradicting or undermining one another's ideas, and revising each other's verse. The result is, as Pessoa said he aspired to create, 'an entire literature', not just one man's oeuvre. Eliot attacked the notion of biography; Pessoa shattered in practice the very concept of authorial biography and voice.

For translators of Pessoa the difficulties are immense. To date, in English, though some have succeeded in transmitting fluently one or even two voices, they invariably fail to effect a convincing rendition of the others. Often a translator feels more akin in spirit and idiom to one *persona* than to the others; and he is the one who is translated while the others are merely interpreted. By concentrating on Pessoa himself, the translators of the present selection have avoided the impossible strain of attempting to match the glossolalia of the collective of heteronyms and orthonym and have poetically presented the English-speaking public with a faithful version of the most confounding and un-self-revealing of the *personae*. At the same time, the

11

reader is made to 'feel' the verse, as in 'This' Pessoa recommends the reader should react to his poems.

Moreover, the translators have organised a selection which is representative of Pessoa's themes and styles, shows an evolution in his poetry, and, with the poem 'Advice', a summing-up. If at times, as in 'Sudden hand of some hidden ghost', the reader intuits the presence of Poe raised to a metaphysical dimension, or, as in 'No, it is not in that lake among crags', a rejection of Wordsworthian Romantic projection of the self into Nature, then these echoes should be trusted, for Pessoa's allusions are usually to literature in English, his avowed favourite. He was steeped in that tradition and the English language, and produced a large body of verse and critical prose in it. His 'ultra-Shakespearean Shakespeareanisms', as one critic dubbed his *35 Sonnets*, written in English, provide an example of how a Portuguese could more convincingly 'forge' a literary tradition, through a masterly command of Elizabethan English, than could Elizabeth Barrett Browning with her feigned translations *Sonnets from the Portuguese*.

But Pessoa would have welcomed translations, for this is how he himself produced much of his verse. Lines of an English original often become his lines in Portuguese, or whole poems. Like Joyce, Pound, Eliot, Borges and other Modernists, he is a multilingual writer. This cross-linguistic facility is one of the very marks of Modernism. Another is, as in Yeats, a theosophical current, to be seen in the first five poems in this volume where there is a plasticity on the part of the *tabula rasa* which is the poetic 'I', which in the last two of these poems asserts its capacity for self-irony. This ultimate insight into Self and into Self's self-deceptions becomes the constant of those poems which deal with the problem of Being and Non-being. In the title-poem for this selection, Being is portrayed as a passionate, only too carnal, seducer for whom the poet longs. However, it is Non-being viewed affirmatively, dispassionately, which is Pessoa's aesthetic goal: 'Free from my own arousal,/ Serious about what is not.'

Indeed, it is this phrasing of negations in an affirmative manner which is at the core of much of the semantic and syntactical 'oddity' of Pessoa's language: 'It is not because . . . ', or 'I don't know what it was which wasn't.' The poem 'I sleep' is an intellectual and a syntactical conundrum, semantic and philosophical paradox being Pessoa's means of undermining all certitude, the nature of collective history or of Dom Sebastian's madness. When given the voyeuristic opportunity to glimpse the open book 'which will never tell' that there is no certitude, the poet looks 'without reading' because that very negation also would be a certitude. The grief expressed towards the stars is as towards the fixity of Being. In the end, Non-being, like non-personality, is the dynamic of existence and of gardening: 'Where no one will see it, plant nothing.'

To maintain the surprise of Being, it is necessary to follow Pessoa's final 'Advice' and retain, walled within our Selves, a bower where there will always flourish a child-like inability to comprehend. That is why Pessoa, in the very demonstrative 'This' – one of his manifesto-poems – orders the reader to 'feel', while the poet confabulates his ideas, images and syntax. It is naive, even primitive awe, not understanding, that Pessoa magically and ludically conjures, with the illusion of syntax, imagery and lyricism, so that there will always be a new sensation of surprise in his language and his *persona*, the mask that is one more voice. As he articulated in English in one of his 'ultra-Shakespearean' sonnets:

'How many masks wear we, and undermasks,
Upon our countenance of soul, and when,
If for self-sport the soul itself unmasks,
Knows it the last mask off and the face plain?
. . .
And, when a thought would unmask our soul's
    masking,
Itself goes not unmasked to the unmasking.'

Jaime H. da Silva
University of Puerto Rico
at Río Piedras

Translators' Preface

We have rendered only poems written by Pessoa under his own name, because these are the poems where, we feel, he is most 'at home' (that is to say, estranged).

Translation is a desire and pursuit of the whole, but it may be that Pessoa, now, is as untranslatable as, say, most of Pushkin. When Geoffrey Hill seeks to write more from the heart than is typical of contemporary English poetry, he attributes these poems to an invented *Spanish* poet, Sebastian Arrurruz, 1868–1922, as if – after *The Waste Land* – such licence, in his own voice, would be embarrassing. (In fact *The Waste Land* can now more easily be seen, since the publication of the original drafts, as the profoundly confessional poem it is, 'the relief' – as Eliot himself said – 'of a personal . . . grouse against life'.) Christopher Reid, similarly, invents an East European, female poet – Katerina Brac.

Pessoa addresses us with an oblique, sad and schizoid, directness (oblique because of the nature and complexity of the issues at stake), a metaphysical candour, in spite of what he claims in 'This', which in any case might be more relevant to his heteronymous poems. 'This', like Eliot's similar pronunciamentos on the extinction of personality in poetry (perhaps the same poker-faced Eliot who, sniggering up his sleeve, put on make-up at parties), seems to us the self-protective stratagem of a publicly reticent man who was subjected to an Anglo-Saxon education. His poems, in our opinion, come from the 'heart' – or what he calls the 'soul' – as well as from a rigorous mind.

We know that others disagree, believing 'Fernando Pessoa himself' to be only another creation or fiction. (Pessoa wrote, in English, as early as 1916:

15

'Sincerity is the one great artistic crime. Insincerity is the second greatest. The great artist should never have a really fundamental and sincere opinion about life. But that should give him the capacity to feel sincere, nay, to be absolutely sincere about anything for a certain length of time – that length of time, say, which is necessary for a poem to be conceived and written.')

Anyone dismayed by our versions and their occasional oddity (we wanted to echo Pessoa's) may refer here to his texts and, at least if he knows Latin, discover something of Pessoa for himself. One should be aware, however, that Portuguese, though a Romance language, isn't *heard* as if it's one. It has struck Peter Rickard's ears as 'far richer in vowel sounds' than Spanish or Italian, while lacking the 'crisply articulated, staccato quality' of those languages and sounding 'curiously muffled.'*

Mandelstam wrote, about Dante, of 'the infantile aspect of Italian phonetics, its beautiful child-like quality, its closeness to infant babbling . . . ' If this puts us in mind of Pessoa's language rather than of Portuguese in general, it must be because of the impact of English on a poet who first wrote in that language; for Pessoa simplified Portuguese via his South African English (while at the same time making it more complex semantically), and his Portuguese is less baroque than other poets' of the period. But none of this makes it any easier to translate Pessoa *into* English, a language (at least, since Chaucer) more sophisticated-sounding, more abstract, and less easily rhymable. Nor does it help that, in the poems under his own name, he used strictly traditional forms.

J. G. and C. de A. M.

* Fernando Pessoa, *Selected Poems*, edited and translated by Peter Rickard, Edinburgh University Press, 1971.

Twenty-five poems

Não sou eu quem descrevo. Eu sou a tela
E oculta mão colora alguém em mim.
Pus a alma no nexo de perdê-la
E o meu princípio floresceu em Fim.

Que importa o tédio que dentro em mim gela,
E o leve Outono, e as galas, e o marfim,
E a congruência da alma que se vela
Com os sonhados pálios de cetim?

Disperso . . . E a hora como um leque fecha-se . . .
Minha alma é um arco tendo ao fundo o mar . . .
O tédio? A mágoa? A vida? O sonho? Deixa-se . . .

E, abrindo as asas sôbre Renovar,
A êrma sombra do vôo começado
Pestaneja no campo abandonado . . .

(*Passos da Cruz*, XI; 1914–16)

It is not I whom I depict. I am the canvas, a hidden hand
Colours somebody on me.
I placed my soul within the bond of losing it,
And my beginning flowered as an End.

What matters the tedium which turns to ice within,
And the weightless autumn, pomp and ivory,
Or the coherence of the soul which keeps its vigil
Behind the dreamt-of canopies of satin?

I disperse . . . And the hour closes like a fan . . .
My soul is an arch having the sea as its end . . .
Tedium? Sorrow? Life? Dream? They are left behind . . .

And, opening wings above Renewal,
The lonely shadow of the flight begun
Blinks on the abandoned field . . .

(*Stations of the Cross*, XI; 1914–16)

Emissário de um rei desconhecido
Eu cumpro informes instruções de além,
E as bruscas frases que aos meus lábios vêm
Soam-me a um outro e anômalo sentido . . .

Inconscientemente me divido
Entre mim e a missão que o meu ser tem,
E a glória do meu Rei dá-me o desdém
Por êste humano povo entre quem lido . . .

Não sei se existe o Rei que me mandou.
Minha missão será eu a esquecer,
Meu orgulho o deserto em que em mim estou . . .

Mas há! Eu sinto-me altas tradições
De antes de tempo e espaço e vida e ser . . .
Já viram Deus as minhas sensações . . .

(*Passos da Cruz*, XIII; 1914–16)

Emissary of an unknown king,
I fulfil unformed instructions from beyond
And on my lips brusque phrases sound
As if they have an alien, other meaning . . .

I divide myself, unknowingly,
Between a mission that my being has, and me,
And the glory of my King enables me to flail
The human-beings among whom I travail . . .

Whether the King exists who sent me I don't know.
My mission will be my forgetting of it,
My pride the desert where I am. But – oh! –

He does! In me I sense illustrious traditions
From before time and space and life and being . . .
Already God has been glimpsed in my sensations . . .

(*Stations of the Cross*, XIII; 1914–16)

Não sei, ama, onde era,
Nunca o saberei . . .
Sei que era primavera
E o jardim do rei . . .
(Filha, quem o soubera! . . .).

Que azul tão azul tinha
Ali o azul do céu!
Se eu não era a rainha
Por que era tudo meu?
(Filha, quem o adivinha?).

E o jardim tinha flôres
De que não me sei lembrar . . .
Flôres de tantas côres . . .
Penso e fico a chorar . . .
(Filha, os sonhos são dores . . .).

Qualquer dia viria
Qualquer coisa a fazer
Tôda aquela alegria
Mais alegria nascer
(Filha, o resto é morrer . . .).

Conta-me contos, ama . . .
Todos os contos são
Êsse dia, e jardim e a dama
Que eu fui nessa solidão . . .

(1916)

I don't know, *ama*,* where it was,
I shall never know . . .
I know it was spring
And the garden of the king . . .
(Child, if one could know! . . .)

What a blue so blue it had,
There, the blue of the sky!
If I was not a Queen,
Why was everything mine?
(Child, who can guess?)

And the garden had flowers
Which I can't recall . . .
Flowers so glowing . . .
I think and am left crying . . .
(Child, dreams are sorrows . . .)

Some day would come,
Something making
More joy
Of all that joy
(Child, the rest is death . . .)

Tell me stories, *ama* . . .
All the stories are
That day, and the garden and lady
Which I was in that solitude . . .

(1916)

* *ama*: wet-nurse, nursemaid.

Súbita mão de algum fantasma oculto
Entre as dobras da noite e do meu sono
Sacode-me e eu acordo, e no abandono
Da noite não enxergo gesto ou vulto.

Mas um terror antigo, que insepulto
Trago no coração, como de um trono
Desce e se afirma meu senhor e dono
Sem ordem, sem meneio e sem insulto.

E eu sinto a minha vida de repente
Prêsa por uma corda de Inconsciente
A qualquer mão noturna que me guia.

Sinto que sou ninguém salvo um sombra
De um vulto que não vejo e que me assombra,
E em nada existo como a treva fria.

(1917)

Sudden hand of some hidden ghost
Among the folds of night and of my sleep
Shakes me awake, and in the forsakenness of night
I glimpse neither gesture nor shape.

But an ancient terror, unburied in my heart,
Descends from its throne
To affirm itself my lord and master:
Without order, without nod, without insult.

And I feel my life all of a sudden
Caught by a rope of unawareness
In some nocturnal hand which guides me.

I feel that I am no one but a shadow
Of a shape I cannot see which haunts me,
And I exist in nothing like the cold dark.

(1917)

25

Abdicação

Toma-me, ó noite eterna, nos teus braços
E chama-me teu filho. Eu sou um rei
Que voluntàriamente abandonei
O meu trono de sonhos e cansaços.

Minha espada, pesada a braços lassos,
Em mãos viris e calmas entreguei;
E meu cetro e coroa, – eu os deixei
Na antecâmara, feitos em pedaços.

Minha cota de malha, tão inútil,
Minhas esporas, de um tinir tão fútil,
Deixei-as pela fria escadaria.

Despi a realeza, corpo e alma,
E regressei à noite antiga e calma
Como a paisagem ao morrer do dia.

(1920–21)

Abdication

Take me in your arms, eternal night,
And call me your son. I am a king
Who voluntarily abandoned
A throne of weariness and dreams.

My sword, a burden to exhausted arms,
I surrendered into calm and manly hands,
And my crown and sceptre I discarded
In the antechamber, shattered.

My redundant coat of mail,
Spurs of barren jangling,
I left along the cold grand-stairway.

I divested royalty from body and soul.
Back now to the calm and ancient night,
Like landscape at the dying of a day.

(1920–21)

Feliz dia para quem é
O igual do dia,
E no exterior azul que vê
Simples confia!

O azul do céu faz pena a quem
Não pode ser
Na alma um azul do céu também
Com que viver

Ah, e se o verde com que estão
Os montes quedos
Pudesse haver no coração
E em seus segredos!

Mas vejo quem devia estar
Igual do dia
Insciente e sem querer passar.
Ah, a ironia

De só sentir a terra e o céu
Tão belos ser
Quem de si sente que perdeu
A alma p'ra os ter!

(1921)

Happy day
For him who is the equal of the day
And trusts, in his simplicity,
In the blue exterior he sees!

The blue of the sky saddens him
Who cannot also in his soul
Be a blue of the sky
To be alive.

Ah, if the green with which the hills
Are tranquil
Could be in the heart
And in its riddles!

But now I see
That he who'd be the equal of the day
Is ignorant and lacks a craving to enjoy.
Ah, the irony

That only he feels earth and sky
Miraculous
Who feels he's lost
The soul to own them!

(1921)

Dorme enquanto eu velo . . .
Deixa-me sonhar . . .
Nada em mim é risonho.
Quero-te para sonho,
Não para te amar.

A tua carne calma
É fria em meu querer.
Os meus desejos são cansaços.
Nem quero ter nos braços
Meu sonho do teu ser.

Dorme, dorme, dorme,
Vaga em teu sorrir . . .
Sonho-te tão atento
Que o sonho é encantamento
E eu sonho sem sentir.

(1921)

Sleep while I watch . . .
Let me dream . . .
There is no laughter in me.
I want you for a dream,
Not to love you.

Your calm flesh
Cold in my desire,
My cravings are wearinesses.
I do not want my dream of your existence
In my arms.

Sleep, sleep, sleep,
Floating in your smiles . . .
I dream you so carefully
That dream is enchantment
And I dream without feeling.

(1921)

Trila na noite uma flauta. É de algum
Pastor? Que importa? Perdida
Série de notas vaga e sem sentido nenhum.
Como a vida.

Sem nexo ou princípio ou fim ondeia
A ária alada.
Pobre ária fora de música e de voz, tão cheia
De não ser nada!

Não há nexo ou fio por que se lembre aquela
Ária, ao parar;
E já ao ouvi-la sofro a saudade dela
E o quando cessar.

(1921)

Epitáfio desconhecido

Quanta mais alma
Por mais que a alma ande no amplo informe,
A ti, seu lar anterior, do fundo
Da emoção regressou, ó Cristo, e dorme
Nos braços cujo amor é o fim do mundo.

(1929)

A flute trills in the night. A shepherd's?
What does it matter? Lost
Series of notes – senseless, vague,
Like living.

The winged aria undulates
Without coherence, beginning or end.
Poor aria, outside music and voice, so full
Of being nothing!

There's no link or thread by which to recall
That aria, when it ceases;
And already, while listening, I long for it
And suffer from its stopping.

(1921)

Unknown epitaph

How many more souls,
However much the soul may wander in the ample
      shapelessness,
Came back to you, their previous home,
From the deeps of emotion, o Christ, and sleep
In the arms whose love is the world's goal.

(1929)

Dá a surpresa de ser.
É alta, de um louro escuro.
Faz bem só pensar em ver
Seu corpo meio maduro.

Seus seios altos parecem
(Se ela estivesse deitada)
Dois montinhos que amanhecem
Sem ter que haver madrugada.

E a mão do seu braço branco
Assenta em palmo espalhado
Sobre a saliência do flanco
Do seu relevo tapado.

Apetece como um barco.
Tem qualquer coisa de gomo.
Meu Deus, quando é que eu embarco?
Ó fome, quando é que eu como?

(1930)

She brings the surprise of being.
She is tall, of a dark blond.
It does good only to think of seeing
Her almost ripe body.

If she lay down,
Her high breasts would seem
Two little hills which dawn
Without need for twilight.

And the hand is spread –
Her white arm's fief –
On the salience of a flank
Of her clothed relief.

Enticing as a boat;
Like a piece of lemon.
When, God, shall I embark?
When, hunger, eat?

(1930)

Desfaze a mala feita pra a partida!
    Chegaste a ousar a mala?
Que importa? Desesperas ante a ida
    Pois tudo a ti te iguala.

Sempre serás o sonho de ti mesmo.
    Vives tendando ser,
Papel rasgado de um intento, a êsmo
    Atirado ao descrer.

Como as correias cingem
    Tudo o que vais levar!
Mas é só a mala e não a ida
    Que há de sempre ficar!

[Como as correias cingem, quase estala
    Tudo o que vais levar!
Mas é só a mala e não a vida na mala
    Que há de sempre ficar!*]

(1931)

*As printed by José Aguilar, São Paulo, 1960.

Unpack the bags got ready for leaving!
Did you really risk a suitcase?
What does it matter? In the face of departure you despair,
Because all's the same to you.

Always you'll be your dream of yourself.
You live trying to be –
Torn paper of an attempt, at random
Hurled towards belieflessness.

How the straps bind
Everything you intend to take!
But it's only the suitcase and not the going
That will always stay!

[How the straps bind, everything you intend to take
        Almost bursts!
But it's only the suitcase – not the life in the suitcase –
        That will always stay!]

(1931)

Bem, hoje que estou só e posso ver
    Com o poder de ver do coração
Quanto não sou, quanto não posso ser,
    Quanto, se o fôr, serei em vão,

Hoje, vou confessar, quero sentir-me
    Definitivamente ser ninguém,
E de mim mesmo, altivo, demitir-me
    Por não ter procedido bem.

Falhei a tudo, mas sem galhardias,
    Nada fui, nada ousei e nada fiz,
Nem colhi nas urtigas dos meus dias
    A flor de parecer feliz.

Mas fica sempre, porque o pobre é rico
    Em qualquer cousa, se procurar bem,
A grande indiferença com que fico.
    Escrevo-o para o lembrar bem.

(1931)

Well, now that I am alone and can see
    With the heart's power to discern
How much I am not, how much I cannot be,
    How much, if I became it, I shall be in vain,

Now, I will confess, I want to feel
    Once and for all I am no one,
And proudly to resign from myself
    For not having acted well.

I failed in everything, though without trying;
    I have been nothing, dared nothing, done nothing,
Nor did I pluck from the nettles of my days
    The flower of seeming-happiness.

But there always remains, because whoever is poor
    Is rich in something, if one looks properly,
The great indifference which is left me.
    I note this to remember it without fail.

(1931)

Vejo passar os barcos pelo mar,
As velas, como asas do que vejo
Trazem-me um vago e íntimo desejo
De ser quem fui, sem eu saber que foi.
Por isso tudo lembra o meu ser lar,
E, porque o lembra, quanto sou me dói.

(1932)

Não, não é nesse lago entre rochedos,
Nem nesse extenso e espúmeo beira-mar,
Nem da floresta ideal cheia de mêdos
Que me fito a mim mesmo e vou pensar.

É aqui, neste quarto de uma casa,
Aqui entre paredes sem paisagem,
Que vejo o romantismo, que foi asa
Do que ignorei de mim, seguir viagem.

É em nós que há os lagos todos e as florestas
Se vemos claro no que somos, é
Não porque as ondas quebrem as arestas
Verdes em branco [. . .]

(1932)

I see the boats go by along the sea.
Their sails, like wings of what I see, bring
A vague and intimate desire for me to be again
Who I was then, although I do not know
Exactly what that was. So everything
Brings back my being as a home
And, recalling this, what I am is pain.

(1932)

No, it is not in that lake among crags,
Nor on that expansive and foaming sea-shore,
Nor in the ideal forest full of fears
That I watch myself and go to ponder.

It is here, in this room of a house,
Here among walls without landscape,
That I see romanticism – wing
Of what I didn't know of myself – take its flight.

It is in us that there are all the lakes and forests
If we see clearly into what we are,
It is not because the waves may break
The green blank edges [. . .]

(1932)

Isto

Dizem que finjo ou minto
Tudo que escrevo. Não.
Eu simplesmente sinto
Com a imaginação.
Não uso o coração.

Tudo o que sonho ou passo,
O que me falha ou finda,
É como que um terraço
Sobre outra coisa ainda.
Essa coisa é que é linda.

Por isso escrevo em meio
Do que não está ao pé,
Livre do meu enleio,
Sério do que não é.
Sentir? Sinta quem lê!

(1930–33)

This

They say that I pretend – or lie –
All that I write.
No. I simply feel
With the imagination,
Do not use the heart.

Everything I go through or dream,
Everything that fails me or ends,
Is like a terrace
Over something else.
That is what's beautiful.

That's why I write in the middle
Of what isn't near,
Free from my own arousal,
Serious about what is not.
Feel? Let the reader feel!

(1930–33)

Dom Sebastião, Rei de Portugal

Louco, sim, louco, porque quis grandeza
Qual a Sorte a não dá.
Não coube em mim minha certeza;
Por isso onde o areal está
Ficou meu ser que houve, não o que há.

Minha loucura, outros que me a tomem
Com o que nela ia.
Sem a loucura que é o homem
Mais que a besta sadia,
Cadáver adiado que procria?

(1933)

Dom Sebastian, King of Portugal

Mad, yes, mad, because I desired greatness
Such as Fate does not give.
I couldn't contain my certainty within me;
That's why, where the sandy shore is,
My being-that-was remained – not the one-that-is.*

My madness, let others accept it from me,
And all that it contained.
Without madness what is man
Other than a healthy animal,
An adjourned and procreating corpse?

(1933)

* 'the one-that-is': his legend, which survives.
From Sebastian's devastating defeat, in his holy
war against the emperor of Morocco, at
Alcazar-Kebir in 1578, there arose the
enduring legend that the king would one day
return as a saviour of his people.

O que me dói não é
O que há no coração
Mas essas coisas lindas
Que nunca existirão . . .

São as formas sem forma
Que passam sem que a dor
As possa conhecer
Ou as sonhar o amor.

São como se a tristeza
Fosse árvore e, uma a uma,
Caíssem suas folhas
Entre o vestígio e a bruma.

(1933)

What hurts me is not
What is in the heart
But those beautiful things
Which will never be.

They are the forms without form
That go by without pain
Being able to know
Or love to dream them.

They are as if sadness
Were a tree and, one by one,
Its leaves were falling
Between the trace and mist.

(1933)

Quando era criança
Vivi, sem saber,
Só para hoje ter
Aquela lembrança.

É hoje que sinto
Aquilo que fui.
Minha vida flui,
Feita do que minto.

Mas nesta prisão,
Livro único, leio
O sorriso alheio
De quem fui então.

(1933)

Durmo. Se sonho, ao despertar não sei
Que coisas eu sonhei.
Durmo. Se durmo sem sonhar, desperto
Para um espaço aberto
Que não conheço, pois que despertei
Para o que inda não sei.
Melhor é nem sonhar nem não sonhar
E nunca despertar.

(1933)

When I was a child
I lived unknowing
In order now to own
This memory of then.

Today I sense
What then I was.
Now my life goes on,
Made of my pretences.

But in this prison,
My only book, I read
The smile of someone else,
Of who I was then.

(1933)

I sleep. If I dream, when I awake I do not know
What things I dreamt. So
I sleep. If I sleep dreamlessly, I awake
Into an open space which I do not recognise,
Since I have wakened now
To what I still don't know.
Better neither to dream nor not to dream
And never to awake.

(1933)

Houve um ritmo no meu sono.
Quando acordei o perdi.
Porque saí do abandono
De mim mesmo, em que vivi?

Não sei que era o que não era.
Sei que suave me embalou,
Como se o embalar quisera
Tornar-me outra vez quem sou.

Houve uma música finda
Quando acordei de a sonhar.
Mas não morreu: dura ainda
No que me faz não pensar.

(1934)

There was a rhythm in my sleep.
When I woke up I lost it.
Why did I step out of this abandon of my self
Inside which I lived?

I don't know what it was which wasn't.
I know it lulled me softly,
As if the lulling longed
To turn me into who I am again.

There was a music interrupted
When I woke up from dreaming it.
But the music didn't die: it still flows on
In what stops me thinking.

(1934)

Montes, e a paz que há neles, pois são longe . . .
Paisagens, isto é, ninguém . . .
Tenho a alma feita para ser de um monge
Mas não me sinto bem.

Se eu fosse outro, fora outro. Assim
Aceito o que me dão,
Como quem espreita para um jardim
Onde os outros estão.

Que outros? Não sei. Há no sossego incerto
Uma paz que não há,
E eu fito sem o ler o livro aberto
Que nunca mo dirá . . .

(1934)

Hills, and the peace in them, for they are far away . . .
Landscapes – that is, no one . . .
I have a soul made to be a monk's
But am not at ease.

If I were other, I would be someone else. As it is,
I accept what's given me,
Like someone who peeps into a garden
Where others are.

Which others? I don't know. In the unsure quiet
Is a peace which isn't.
And I look, without reading, at the open book
Which will never tell me . . .

(1934)

Foi um momento
O em que pousaste
Sobre o meu [braço,]
Num movimento
Mais de cansaço
Que pensamento,
A tua mão
E a retiraste.
Senti ou não?

Não sei. Mas lembro
E sinto ainda
Qualquer memória
Fixa e corpórea
Onde pousaste
A mão que teve
Qualquer sentido
Incompreendido,
Mas tão de leve! . . .

Tudo isto é nada,
Mas numa estrada
Como é a vida
Há uma coisa
Incompreendida . . .

Sei eu se quando
A tua mão
Senti pousando
Sobre o meu braço,
E um pouco, um pouco,
No coração,
Não houve um ritmo
Novo no espaço?

It was then –
When you laid your hand
On my arm,
More in weariness
Than deliberation,
And took it away again.
Did I feel it?

I don't know. But I do remember,
And still feel,
Some firm and corporeal
Memory
Of where you laid your hand
(It had a meaning
One could not understand),
But so lightly! . . .

All this is nothing,
But on a road
Such as life
There is a thing
That can't be understood . . .

Do I know whether or not,
When I felt your hand
On my arm and –
A little –
On my heart,
There was a new rhythm in space?

Como se tu,
Sem o querer,
Em mim tocasses
Para dizer
Qualquer mistério,
Súbito e etéreo,
Que nem soubesses
Que tinha ser.

Assim a brisa
Nos ramos diz
Sem o saber
Uma imprecisa
Coisa feliz.

(1934)

As if you,
Without meaning to,
Had touched me
To say
Some mystery –
Surprising, ethereal –
Unknowingly.

So the breeze
On the branches
Speaks, without knowing,
An imprecise
Thrilling thing.

(1934)

Tenho dó das estrêlas
Luzindo há tanto tempo,
Há tanto tempo . . .
Tenho dó delas.

Não haverá um cansaço
Das coisas,
De tôdas as coisas,
Como das pernas ou de um braço?

De um cansaço de existir,
De ser,
Só de ser,
O ser triste brilhar ou sorrir . . .

Não haverá, enfim,
Para as coisas que são,
Não a morte, mas sim
Uma outra espécie de fim,
Ou uma grande razão –
Qualquer coisa assim
Como um perdão?

(1934)

I grieve for the stars
Glowing for so long,
For so long.
I grieve.

Won't there be a tiredness
Of things,
Of all things,
As of the legs or an arm?

A tiredness of existing,
Of being,
Just of being,
Of being sad to shine or smile . . .

Won't there be, at last,
For the things that are,
Not death, but rather
Another kind of ending,
Or a great justice – something
A bit like a pardon?

(1934)

As Ilhas Afortunadas

Que voz vem no som das ondas
Que não é a voz do mar?
É a voz de alguém que nos fala,
Mas que, se escutamos, cala,
Por ter havido escutar.

E só se, meio dormindo,
Sem saber de ouvir ouvimos,
Que ela nos diz a esperança
A que, como uma criança
Dormente, a dormir sorrimos.

São ilhas afortunadas,
São terras sem ter lugar,
Onde o Rei mora esperando.
Mas, se vamos despertando,
Cala a voz, e há só o mar.

(1934)

The Fortunate Islands

What voice comes in the sound of the waves
Which isn't the voice of the sea?
It is the voice of someone who speaks to us
But who, if we listen, is silent,
For having been listened to.

And only if, half-sleeping,
We hear without knowing we hear,
Does it tell us the hope
At which, like a sleeping child,
We smile as we sleep.

They are fortunate islands,
Unmappable lands,
Where the king dwells, waiting.
But if we start to awake
The voice is silent, and there is only the sea.

(1934)

Conselho

Cerca de grandes muros quem te sonhas.
Depois, onde é visível o jardim
Através do portão de grade dada,
Põe quantas flôres são as mais risonhas,
Para que te conheçam só assim.
Onde ninguém o vir não ponhas nada.

Faze canteiros como os que outros têm,
Onde os olhares possam entrever
O teu jardim como lho vais mostrar.
Mas onde és teu, e nunca o vê ninguém
Deixa as flôres, que vêm do chão crescer
E deixa as ervas naturais medrar.

Faze de ti um duplo ser guardado;
E que ninguém, que veja e fite, possa
Saber mais que um jardim de quem tu és –
Um jardim ostensivo e reservado,
Por trás do qual a flor nativa roça
A erva tão pobre que nem tu a vês . . .

(1935)

Advice

Surround with tall walls whoever you dream you are.
Then, where the garden can be seen
Through the gate with its bestowing bars,
Place whatever flowers are the most smiling,
So they may know you only like that.
Where no one will see it, plant nothing.

Make flowerbeds like the ones other people have
Where glances may glimpse your garden,
Such as you are going to show it to them.
But where you are yours and it is seen by no one,
Let the flowers that come from the ground grow
And let the natural grasses flourish.

Make of yourself a two-fold guarded being;
And may no one who might see or watch
Know more of who you are than a garden –
A garden conspicuous and set-apart,
Behind which the native flower brushes
Grass so poor that not even you can see it . . .

(1935)